SCHOLASTIC

Number Tales

1 2 3 TEACHING GUIDE

by Judy Nayer

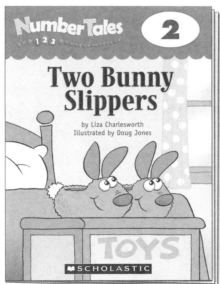

New York • Toronto • London • Auckland • Sydney •
New Delhi • Mexico City • Hong Kong • Buenos Aires

Cover design by Maria Lilja
Interior design by Grafica
Activity sheet illustrations by Doug Jones and Jason Robinson. Mini-book illustrations by Hector Borlasca, Maxie Chambliss, Doug Jones, Anne Kennedy, Kelly Kennedy, Stephen Lewis, Daniel J. Mahoney, Brenda Sexton, and Jackie Snider.
ISBN: 0–439–69028–5

Table of Contents

Welcome to *NumberTales!* 4

Teaching the Standards 5

Using the Program 7

Classroom Activities 15

The Mini-Books & Practice Pages

Number 0: Zero Spots 17

Number 1: One Little Egg 23

Number 2: Two Bunny Slippers 29

Number 3: Three Bouncing Balls 35

Number 4: Four Fiddlers 41

Number 5: Five Shiny Apples 47

Number 6: Six Cheers for Ladybug 53

Number 7: Seven Magic Hats 59

Number 8: Eight Legs Are Great 65

Number 9: Nine Bright Pennies 71

Number 10: Ten Fingers Can! 77

Number 30: Thirty Mice Are Very Nice 83

Number 100: 100 Wacky Wishes 89

Skip Counting: The Ants Go Marching Two by Two 95

Simple Addition: The Happy Hippos 101

Simple Subtraction: Monkey's Missing Bananas 107

More Reproducibles 113

Welcome to

Learning to count is an exciting accomplishment for any young child. Those numbers that children recite so proudly lead the way to the wondrous world of math—counting, understanding quantity, adding, subtracting, and more.

NumberTales offer a fun and easy way to capitalize on children's natural interest in learning numbers. Each simple, imaginative story focuses on a different number or skill, teaching the numbers 0 to 10, 30, 100, skip counting, simple addition, and simple subtraction. The engaging stories help children build number knowledge and number sense—essential components of early math skills—while providing a language-rich context for these explorations.

Other features in the *NumberTales* program are:

- a **hide-and-seek counting activity** at the end of each story that invites children to find sets of objects in an illustrated scene for the featured number or skill (see pages 14–15 of picture books).

- an **easy-to-learn rhyming cheer** designed to help children remember "how many" stand for each number and reinforce math concepts as well as to celebrate learning through chanting and movement (see page 16 of picture books).

- **teaching notes and activity suggestions** to help you introduce the *NumberTales*, build on each story's math lesson, strengthen children's numeracy skills, and assess students' progress (see pages 7–16 of this teaching guide).

- **reproducible patterns for making mini-book versions of all 16 stories** in the *NumberTales* series (see pages 17–110 of this teaching guide).

- **reproducible practice pages** for each story to give children further exposure to and practice with each number or skill, plus review pages (see pages 21–112 of this teaching guide).

- **reproducible flashcards and spinners** to use again and again in a variety of individual, partner, and group activities (see pages 116–119 of this teaching guide).

Teaching the Standards

The National Council of Teachers of Mathematics (NCTM) and the National Association for the Education of Young Children (NAEYC) affirm that "high-quality, challenging, and accessible mathematics education for three-to-six-year-old children is a vital foundation for future mathematics learning." It is critical that the same "good beginnings" children have been exposed to in learning to read and write be applied to children's early experience in learning math.

The *NumberTales* storybooks, along with the activities and practice pages in this teacher book, are designed to support the recommendations by the NCTM and NAEYC that high-quality mathematics education for 3- to 6-year-olds should:

- enhance children's natural interest in mathematics and their disposition to use it to make sense of their physical and social worlds;

- build on children's varying experiences, including their family, linguistic, and cultural backgrounds; their individual approaches to learning; and their informal knowledge;

- base mathematics curriculum and teaching practices on current knowledge of young children's cognitive, linguistic, physical, and social-emotional development;

- use curriculum and teaching practices that strengthen children's problem-solving and reasoning processes as well as representing, communicating, and connecting mathematical ideas;

- ensure that the curriculum is coherent and compatible with known relationships and sequences of important mathematical ideas;

- provide for children's deep and sustained interaction with key mathematical ideas;

- integrate mathematics with other activities and other activities with mathematics;

- provide ample time, materials, and teacher support for children to engage in play, a context in which they explore and manipulate mathematical ideas with keen interest;

- actively introduce mathematical concepts, methods, and language through a range of appropriate experiences and teaching strategies;

- support children's learning by thoughtfully and continually assessing all children's mathematical knowledge, skills, and strategies.

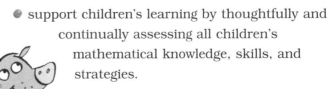

Additionally, the *NumberTales* series supports children in meeting the following NCTM standards and expectations:

NUMBER AND OPERATIONS

Standard	Expectations
Understand numbers, ways of representing numbers, relationships among numbers, and number systems	• count with understanding and recognize "how many" in sets of objects • develop understanding of the relative position and magnitude of whole numbers • develop a sense of whole numbers and represent and use them in flexible ways, including relating, composing, and decomposing numbers • connect number words and numerals to the quantities they represent, using various physical models and representations
Understand meanings of operations and how they relate to one another	• understand various meanings of addition and subtraction of whole numbers and the relationship between the two operations
Compute fluently and make reasonable estimates	• develop and use strategies for whole-number computations, with a focus on addition and subtraction • develop fluency with basic number combinations for addition and subtraction • use a variety of methods and tools to compute

Use the *NumberTales* series to help give children a head start in math and master the following essential skills:

- Count numbers in sequence
- Use one-to-one correspondence to count objects
- Recognize written numerals
- Match numerals to objects in sets
- Write written numerals
- Associate numerals with number words
- Understand *greater than, less than, same*
- Skip count by 2s and 10s
- Count from 0 to 100; read numbers from 0 to 100
- Understand simple addition and subtraction stories
- Add and subtract objects

Using the Program

Learning About Numbers

Many children enter school already able to count and recognize a few numbers. However, being able to say the names of the numbers is not the same as understanding number concepts. At the first stage of counting, children learn to say number names, but not necessarily in order. They might say something like, "One, two, three, five, eleven. . ." At the next stage, children memorize numbers in sequence, but even though they know the correct order, they are still counting by rote.

Children don't really understand counting until they develop the idea that there is a *one-to-one correspondence* between each number name spoken and an object in the set being counted. In counting a set of three toy cars, for example, children point to each car, in turn, as they say, "1, 2, 3." They know that the number name, 3, stands for not only the last car named, but also the whole set of cars. They also know that there is the same number in a set of three toy cars as there are in a set of three cookies or any other three objects. In addition, children learn that three cars are more than two cars, and that the number of cars does not change if their arrangement is changed.

As you help children develop their number sense, keep in mind the following:

- At this age, children may not be able to identify numbers or read number words. They may also not have the fine-motor skills for writing numbers. Don't worry—these abilities will come in time. For now, it is more important that children understand that numbers represent quantities.

- Children need many experiences counting real, concrete objects. These experiences are critical for developing an understanding of numbers. Set up a math center in the classroom and provide a variety of manipulatives for children to use in counting activities.

- For some children, the process of understanding numbers requires more practice and time. These children need additional opportunities counting concrete objects, drawing sets of objects and recording how many, and other hands-on activities.

- Help children understand that math is all around us and we use math every day. Point out important numbers—age, height, address, phone number, numbers on a clock, numbers on a calendar—and encourage children to look for numbers everywhere they go. Incorporate counting into your daily routines by counting books on the shelf, steps to the door, children in a line, blocks in a tower, and so on. Talk about numbers of things as you go through the day so that children see how numbers are used. If anything needs to be counted, have children do so. In addition, encourage children to use the language of math in their activities. For example: *My tower has seven blocks; I can hop five times; There is one cracker for each child.*

- Incorporate learning in a variety of activities to make learning more fun, such as singing a counting song. For example, make two fists and then unfold one finger at a time as you sing: *1 little, 2 little, 3 little children, 4 little 5 little 6 little children, 7 little, 8 little 9 little children, 10 little children right here.* Have children sing and do the movements with you.

- Read a variety of counting books with children, and set up a reading center with counting books so children can explore them on their own. Encourage children to say the number on each page and provide manipulatives for them to use as they count the objects.

- Most important of all, share your excitement and interest and introduce children to the joys of reading and math!

Using the Storybooks

Before Reading

- Introduce the featured number or skill of the *NumberTales* book you are reading with an assortment of quick activities.

- Use a wet sponge to write the featured number on the chalkboard. Can children guess the number before it disappears?

- Write the number on the chalkboard or chart paper. Display a set of objects to match the number. Point to each object as you count it. Repeat, having children count along with you.

- Show children the cover of the book. Ask them to identify the numeral at the top. Have them count the items in the illustration.

- Read aloud the title of the book. Have children use the title and the illustration to make predictions about what the story will be about. Flip the book over and read the story summary on the back cover. Were children's predictions correct?

During Reading

- The first time, read the selected *NumberTales* book aloud all the way through. Let children enjoy the story and get a feel for the language.

- When you reread the story, ask children to stop and count the items on the pages with you. Point to the illustrations as children count along.

- On another reading of the story, have children identify numbers and number words in the story. Encourage children to chime in on the numbers, number words, and any other words they know.

- Provide each child with counters. Have children count out the number of counters needed (for example, three counters for the "3" book). As you read each page of the book, have children point to each counter and count along.

After Reading

- Share the two-page illustration at the end of each *NumberTales* book. Encourage children to find and count the objects in the picture that are named in the text. Challenge them to find additional sets of objects as well.

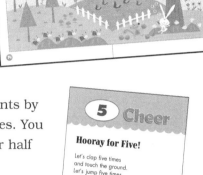

- Have fun with the cheer that accompanies each *NumberTales* book. As you recite the cheer, have children act out the movements by clapping, jumping, and stomping the appropriate number of times. You may wish to have half the class act out the cheer while the other half chants, and then change roles.

Using the Mini-Books

The reproducible mini-books are an excellent way to strengthen children's skills and build a home-school connection. Here are some ideas for using the mini-books both in and out of the classroom:

- After you've read a *NumberTales* story aloud several times, provide children with the reproducible mini-book pattern and help them make their very own copy of the story. Children can then follow along in their mini-books as you read the story again.

● Make audio recordings of the stories and put them in a special listening center. Provide copies of the mini-books so that children can follow along with the tapes.

● Ask each child to bring in a shoebox from home. Then set out a variety of art materials and allow students to decorate the boxes. Children can then use the boxes to house their very own *NumberTales* mini-book. Children will enjoy returning to the stories again and again.

● Let children take home their mini-books to read with family members. Children can "announce" the number your class is currently studying by wearing a special badge (see page 11). The badge can also serve as an invitation to parents and caregivers to read the latest *NumberTales* story with their child. Children and adults can then look around their home for the target number and count things that add up to the target number.

Making the Mini-Books

1. Make double sided copies of the mini-book pages. (You should have two double-sided copies for each one.)

2. Cut the pages in half along the dashed line.

3. Position the pages so that the lettered spreads (A, B, C, D) are face up. Place the B spread on top of the A spread. Then, place the C and D spread on top of those in sequence.

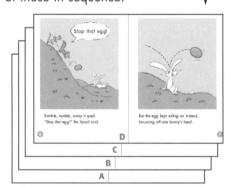

4. Fold the pages in half along the solid line. Make sure all the pages are in the proper order. Staple them together along the book's spine.

Making the Badge

Photocopy the pattern for each child. Trim the badge to size and help children fill in the number of the week. Children can then color the badge. Punch a hole at the top and string with yarn so children can wear the badge around their neck.

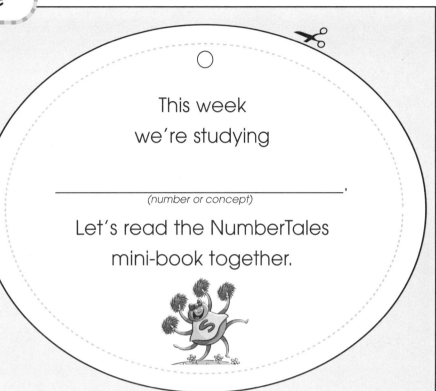

This week
we're studying

_____
(number or concept)

Let's read the NumberTales
mini-book together.

Using the Practice Pages

Each story is followed by two reproducible pages to allow children to practice and reinforce essential numeracy skills. Use the practice pages for whole-group, small-group, or individual work. You might also:

- give practice pages to children to complete at home.
- put copies of the pages in a math center.
- have children create folders in which they collect their completed sheets and bind them into a book.
- include the pages in children's portfolios for informal assessment.

On the first page children:

- identify the numeral at the top and read the number word for that numeral.
- count and color that number of objects on the page to reinforce one-to-one correspondence.
- trace the numeral along guiding gray lines.
- write the numeral themselves.

On the second page children:

- count sets and identify the groups with the target number.

- create sets by drawing or coloring the same number of objects as the target number.

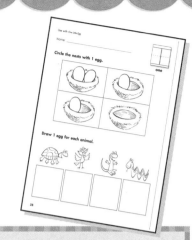

TIPS!

- Point to each item on the page as children count them. This will help children understand the one-to-one correspondence between the objects being counted and their number value.

- Examine the numeral children will be practicing. Write the numeral on the chalkboard or on chart paper and demonstrate its formation. For example: *The numeral 1 starts at the top and makes a stick straight down.*

- Before tracing and writing the numeral using pencil, have children trace the numeral in the air. Start with large numbers and gradually show children how to write smaller air numbers, until they are ready to write the numbers on paper.

- After writing the numeral, have children circle their best number in the row.

- Children may lose track of how many items they have counted. Help children keep track of what has been counted by lightly marking off the ones they've counted with a pencil.

- Note that the practice pages that accompany the books for 100, skip counting, addition, and subtraction are different from the format of the other pages. Be sure to go over the directions with children before asking them to complete these pages.

Using the Review Pages

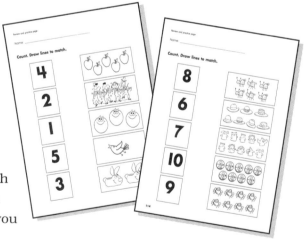

- On pages 113–114 you'll find practice pages for the numbers 1 to 5 and 6 to 10. Copy and distribute these cumulative review pages after completing the practice pages for the number 5 and the practice pages for the number 10. Go over the directions with children before having them complete the page. You may also wish to use these pages with children as you assess their number skills.

- On page 115 you'll find a hundreds chart. Copy and distribute this page after completing the practice pages for the number 100. Use the suggestions that follow for sharing the page with children. You may also wish to use this page with children as you assess their number skills.

● Ask children what pattern they see in each row going down and in each row going diagonally. Ask children if they can find other patterns. As you skip count by tens, have them read along and circle each number in the pattern as you call it out. Have children create a pattern on their papers by coloring each row of ten a different color. You can also use the hundreds chart to practice skip counting by five's and two's.

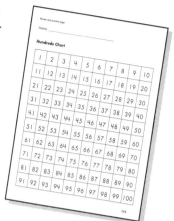

Using the Flashcards

On pages 116–117 you'll find 20 flashcards that can be reproduced and cut apart for a variety of activities. You may also use the flashcards to help you assess children's number knowledge. Here are some ideas to get started:

● Copy and distribute the cards to pairs of children. Children turn all the cards facedown and turn over two at a time, trying to make a match. If they do so, they keep the cards and take another turn; if they do not, they turn the cards back over and the next player has a turn. Use the cards to practice matching numerals and number words to the correct number of stars. Or, copy two sets of the numeral cards or two sets of the star cards and have children make direct matches.

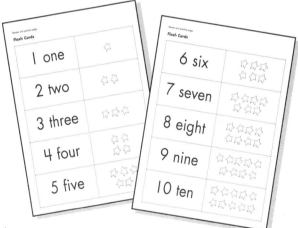

● Have children use the cards individually with manipulatives to practice counting. Distribute the cards and have children match the numeral cards to the star cards. Then have them place one manipulative on each star and count the number of manipulatives on the card. The number counted should equal the numeral printed on the card.

● Make several copies of the star cards and put them in a pile. Have children play in pairs. Each partner picks a card and children count the stars to determine who has the biggest number. The winner takes those two cards.

Using the Spinners

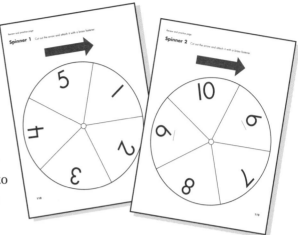

On pages 118–119 you'll find two spinners with five numbers each. Duplicate the pages, then cut out the arrows and attach them to the spinners with a brass fastener. (For more durable spinners, glue the circles and arrows onto tagboard and laminate.) Use the spinners to play number games and to help you assess children's number knowledge. Here are some ideas to get started:

● Have children play with a partner. Children take turns spinning the arrow and reading aloud the number it stops on. Then they show counters or other manipulatives to "make" the number. Children can put the counters in a cup and play until they fill it up, or use any other variation on how to end the game.

● Draw a simple game board on a piece of posterboard. Label "Start" and "Finish" boxes. Give pairs or small groups of children game pieces and have them take turns spinning a number and moving their game piece that many spaces.

● Have children use the 1–5 spinner and manipulatives to create simple addition stories. For example, a child spins a 3 and takes three beans. Next the child spins a 2 and takes two beans. Have the child draw a picture to represent the addition and then dictate a story which you can record on their paper. For example: *I got three beans. I got two more beans. Now I have five beans. 3 beans + 2 beans = 5 beans.*

Assessment

The following suggestions will help you assess children's familiarity with the numbers and number skills presented in the *NumberTales* program. You may use the practice pages, flashcards, and spinners, along with manipulatives, to help determine whether children have mastered these skills.

● Can the child count in sequence?
● Can the child identify the number?
● Can the child count a set of objects showing the number?

- Can the child create a set of objects showing the number?
- Can the child write the number?
- Can the child read the number name?
- Does the child understand concepts of *more, less,* and *same?*
- Can the child use grouping strategies to count larger numbers?
- Can the child skip count by 2's to 20 and by 10's to 100?
- Does the child understand the concepts of simple addition and subtraction?
- Can the child tell simple stories using addition and subtraction?

Classroom Activities

Use these activities to further reinforce and provide hands-on experiences with the math concepts that were introduced in the *NumberTales* books.

NumberTales Around the Room

- Each time you read a *NumberTales* book for the numbers 0 to 10, have a different pair or small group of children make a piece of a number frieze. Have children write the letter on a sheet of drawing paper, draw a picture of the items or characters from the story, and write the story's title. Display on the wall at children's eye level, and add to the frieze with each book you read.

- You can also build a class number line as you count the days in school. Begin on the first day of school, each day writing the next number on a 3" x 5" index card. Tape all the cards in sequence on the wall where the whole class can see. Change colors every ten numbers, or mark the 10's with stickers. On the hundredth day of school, plan a special celebration.

- The number line will be especially useful as you share the *NumberTales* books for 30, 100, skip counting, addition, and subtraction. Have children refer to the number line as you count to 30 in *Thirty Mice Are Very Nice*, skip count by 2's in *The Ants Go Marching Two by Two*, count to 100 and skip count by 10's to 100 in *One Hundred Wacky Wishes*, and add and subtract objects in *The Happy Hippos* and *Monkey's Missing Bananas*.

- Help children learn "greater than" and "less than" by using the number line to play "Mystery Number." Think of a number between 0 and 10 or 0 and 30. Have children take turns guessing. If the number is too large, have them guess a smaller number. If the number is too small, have them guess a larger number.

Number of the Week Invite children to participate in a variety of activities for each number you explore in the *NumberTales* series. Here are some ideas for "Number of the Week":

● Have children explore the number of the week at counting stations using manipulatives such as counters, snap cubes, buttons, sorting animals, pasta, dry cereal, toothpicks, and beans. Display clear jars labeled with the number. Have children count and place the correct number of objects inside the jar; other children can take out the objects and count to check.

● Take a walk around the school or neighborhood and look for the number of the week on bulletin boards, classroom doors, signs, houses, license plates, store windows, and so on. Look for sets of the number in the environment as well. For example, you might see two wheels on a bicycle or four windows on a house. In class, you might make snacks with three raisins on a peanut butter cracker or you might cut apples into six pieces. Go on a scavenger hunt to find collections of objects for the number, such as a jacket with six buttons, four chairs around a table, or a tower with five blocks. Record children's findings and observations on a "Number of the Week" bulletin board.

● Have children glue or draw objects to a piece of construction paper to show the target number, and label their paper with the numeral and number name. Assemble children's number drawings into a book.

Simon Says Fun Have children stand facing you and give them instructions that tell them how many times they should make a certain movement. Tell children that they should only follow the instruction if you say "Simon says" first. Give children instructions that include the number of times they should do each movement, for example: "Simon says clap three times," "Simon says stamp your feet five times," "Take two twirling steps," "Simon says wiggle your hips eight times," and so on.

Addition and Subtraction Tales Have children use two colors of counters, snap cubes, beans, or other manipulatives to act out the addition and subtraction facts in *The Happy Hippos* and *Monkey's Missing Bananas*. Then invite children to make up their own addition and subtraction stories. Model how to tell a story, such as: *There were 4 cookies on the plate. I ate 1 cookie. There are 3 cookies left.* Write the subtraction sentence that tells about the story: 4 – 1 = 3. Provide children with crayons, markers, and paper. Have pairs work together to make up an addition or subtraction story, write the addition fact or subtraction fact that tells about it, and draw a picture to go with it. If children need help, provide the addition or subtraction fact and have them create the story and illustration.

Hooray for Zero!

Let's clap and tap
and touch the ground.
Let's jump and thump
and spin around.
Let's wave and wiggle
and cheer and shout
for a wonderful number
we can't live without:
      ZERO!

Zero Spots

by Liza Charlesworth
Illustrated by Doug Jones

SCHOLASTIC

Ugg had to admit, Sue's words were right.
His spotlessness WAS quite a sight!

Here's Monster Dot.
Does she have spots?
Yes, lots and lots and lots and lots.

A

From that day on, Ugg loved his skin
and never wanted spots again.
Yes, lots of spots do add some spice,
but zero spots sure does look nice.

13

But her friend Ugg, he has none—
not twenty, not ten, not even one.

"Blue like the ocean, blue like the sky,
blue like a blue jay and blueberry pie!"

2

B

11

"Just look in the mirror—
you're brilliant blue!"

Zero spots is just no fun.

After a while, Ugg started to cry.
"I wish I had spots," he said with a sigh.

But Monster Ugg, he still has none—
not thirty, not seven, not even one.
Zero spots is just no fun!

Here's Monster Spike.
Does he have spots?
Yes, lots and lots and lots and lots.

"Don't be sad," said Monster Sue.
"From head to toe, you're special, too."

Here's Monster Sue.
Does she have spots?
Yes, lots and lots and lots and lots.

But Monster Ugg, he still has none—
not a hundred, not two, not even one.
Zero spots is just no fun!

Name: _____

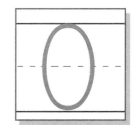

zero

Monster Ugg has 0 spots. Color him blue.

Trace 0.

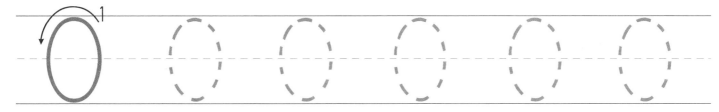

Write 0.

Name: _____

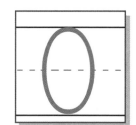

zero

Circle the animals with 0 spots.

Hooray for One!

Let's clap one time
and touch the ground.
Let's jump one time
and spin around.
Let's stomp one time
and cheer and shout
for a wonderful number
we can't live without:
   ONE!

One Little Egg

by Jaime Lucero
Illustrated by Kelly Kennedy

SCHOLASTIC

Then chip! chip! chip!—
the egg broke into bits,
and out popped one robin, lickety-split!

Once upon a time, in a tall oak tree,
sat one little egg, blue as could be.

"Sorry I hurt you," the robin sighed,
"that gust of wind took me for a ride!"
"No problem," said the lizard. "Let's all be friends."
And that is how our story ends.

A

Then, the wind came along with a mighty w-h-o-o-s-h
and gave that one little egg a push.

B

Then lo and behold, it came to a rest—
miles away from its snug little nest.
"Oh no," said the bunny, "I see a crack.
I think we all should take one step back."

Rumble, tumble, away it sped.
"Stop that egg!" the turtle said.

Down, down, down, it dropped like lead,
bouncing off one squirrel's head.

Rumble, tumble, away it sped.
"Stop that egg!" the bunny said.

But the egg kept rolling on instead,
bouncing off one lizard's head.

Then rumble, tumble, away it sped.
"Stop that egg!" the squirrel said.

C

But the egg kept rolling on instead,
bouncing off one turtle's head.

Rumble, tumble, away it sped.
"Stop that egg!" the lizard said.

D

But the egg kept rolling on instead,
bouncing off one bunny's head.

Name: _____

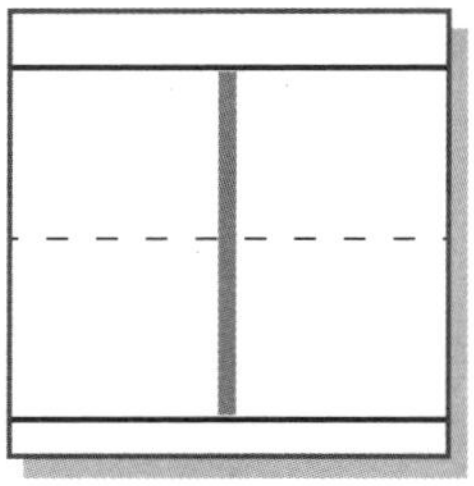

one

Count and color 1 egg.

Trace 1.

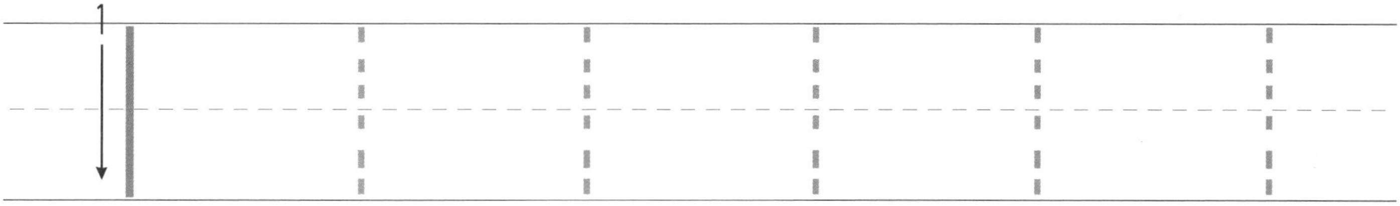

Write 1.

Name: _____

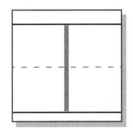

Circle the nests with 1 egg.

one

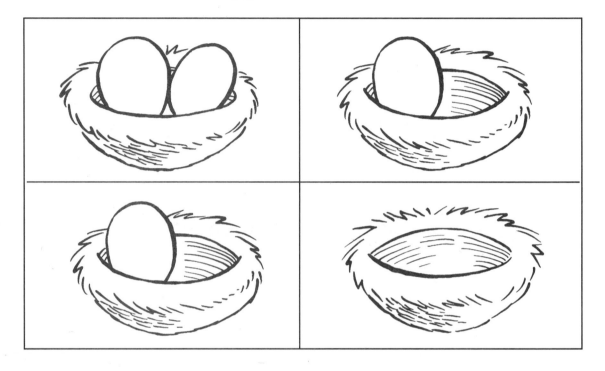

Draw 1 egg for each animal.

Hooray for Two!

Let's clap two times
and touch the ground.
Let's jump two times
and spin around.
Let's stomp two times
and cheer and shout
for a wonderful number
we can't live without:
TWO!

Two Bunny Slippers

by Liza Charlesworth
Illustrated by Doug Jones

SCHOLASTIC

After that, the pair of slippers
hopped back to Lottie's side.

Lottie loved her two slippers,
the left one and the right...

A

They wanted to be ready
when she opened up her eyes.

but when she slipped them off at night—
oh my, was it a sight!

B

then chased his tail in circles
until the break of dawn.

Hank liked those two slippers,
and so he tried them on

You see, that pair of slippers
hopped, hopped around her room.

but the party got exciting

They hopped into a corner
where they made a spider friend,

They chatted with two teddy bears
and gazed up at the moon.

when Hank the cat arrived.

who invited them to a two o'clock tea
with dolls named Ann and Ken.

The cupcakes were amazing,
the carrots were divine...

Name: _____

two

Count and color 2 slippers.

Trace 2.

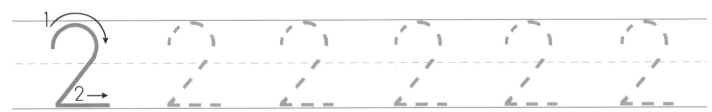

Write 2.

Name: _____

two

Circle the groups with 2.

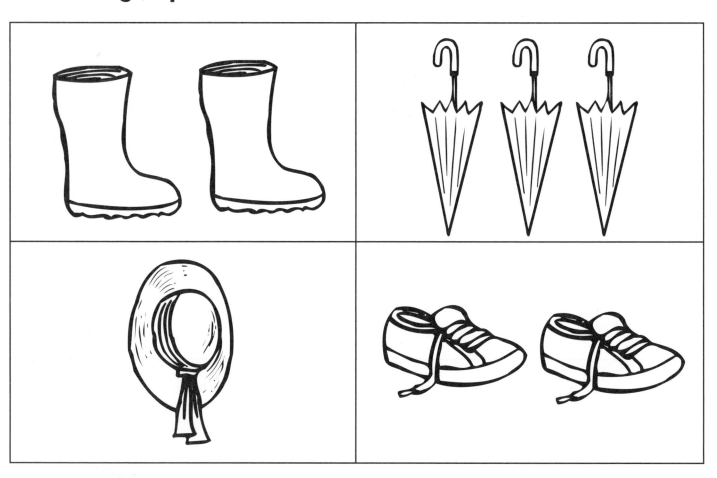

Draw more to make 2.

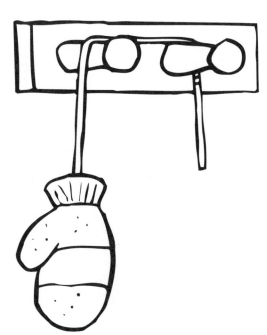

Hooray for Three!

Let's clap three times
and touch the ground.
Let's jump three times
and spin around.
Let's stomp three times
and cheer and shout
for a wonderful number
we can't live without:
THREE!

Three Bouncing Balls

by Liza Charlesworth
Illustrated by Doug Jones

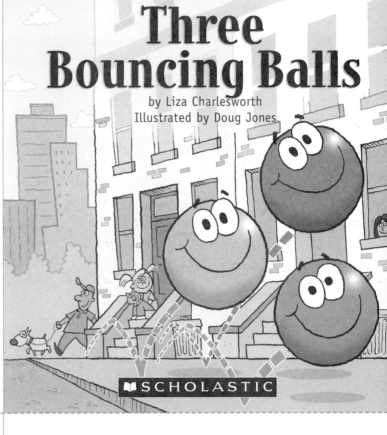

SCHOLASTIC

"One, two, three, let's roll right home

Three bouncing balls—
one red, one green, one blue—

and bounce into our bed."

A

13

slipped off a toy shelf
and got kicked by a shoe.

After that, they were super-sleepy,
so the little red ball said,

2

B

11

Then squeaky clean, they bounced, bounced, bounced
along a garden path.

They bounced out the door
and down a dozen steps.

who scooped them all up—one, two, three!—
and juggled them round and round.

They bounced into a wagon
and the three, they took a ride—

They bounced past the postman
and Mrs. Cadoodle's pets.

C

Then, he dropped them in a fountain
where those three balls had a bath.

bump, bump, bump to the playground,
where they slid down a slippery slide.

D

Next, they bounced beside a singer
and a very silly clown,

Name: _____

three

Count and color 3 balls.

Trace 3.

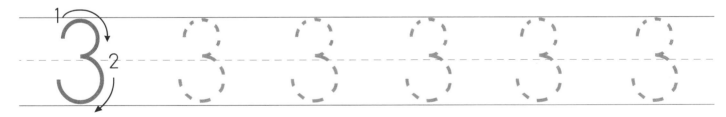

Write 3.

Name: _____

three

Circle the groups with 3.

Draw 3 balls.

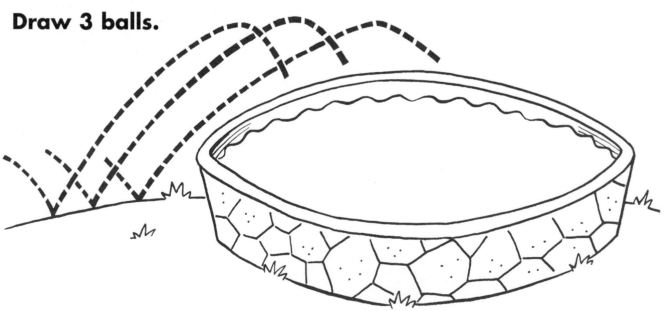

Hooray for Four!

Let's clap four times
and touch the ground.
Let's jump four times
and spin around.
Let's stomp four times
and cheer and shout
for a wonderful number
we can't live without:
FOUR!

Four Fiddlers

by Teddy Slater
Illustrated by Kelly Kennedy

SCHOLASTIC

And that's when the pigs
give the fiddlers a chance
to put down their fiddles . . .

Four fiddlers fiddling a toe-tapping tune.
We're having a barn dance under the moon.

A

and dance, dance, dance, dance!

The first to arrive are four hefty hogs.

They're too tired now
to dance anymore.

B

The dancers dance on
till a quarter to four.

And right behind them
come four dancing dogs.

Whirling and twirling
are four woolly sheep.

Goats, horses, chickens crowd onto the floor.

Four by four, they march through the door.

They dance till they drop
and fall down in a heap.

Fiddle-de-dee! It's time to begin.
Four dandy ducks start off with a spin.

D

Four cows circle round
to the left and the right.
These graceful creatures are quite a sight!

C

Name: _____

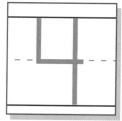

four

Count and color 4 fiddles.

Trace 4.

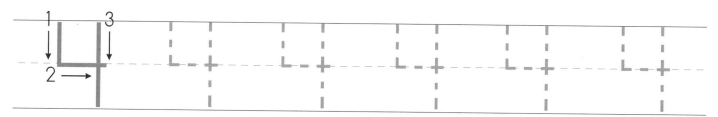

Write 4.

Name: _____

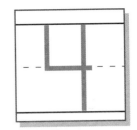

four

Circle the groups with 4.

Color 4 of each.

Hooray for Five!

Let's clap five times
and touch the ground.
Let's jump five times
and spin around.
Let's stomp five times
and cheer and shout
for a wonderful number
we can't live without:
FIVE!

Five Shiny Apples

by Maria Fleming
Illustrated by Brenda Sexton

SCHOLASTIC

Five hungry friends, ready to munch
five shiny apples…

Five shiny apples, ready to crunch.
Who will pick them for their lunch?

A

crunch, crunch, crunch, crunch, crunch!

Along comes rabbit. He wants to try.

B

Soon all five apples fall down in a shower.

So quick as a wink, they make a tall tower.

But those five shiny apples are just too high.

If we all work together, we can get the job done!

Along comes chipmunk, who tells everyone,

But those five shiny apples are just too high.

Along comes turtle. She wants to try.

"If we all work together, we can get the job done!"

C

Along comes bullfrog. He wants to try.
But those five shiny apples are just too high.

Along comes woodchuck. She wants to try.
But those five shiny apples are just too high.

D

Use with *Five Shiny Apples*

Name: ______________________________

5

five

Count and color 5 apples.

Trace 5.

1 3 2 5 5 5 5 5 5

Write 5.

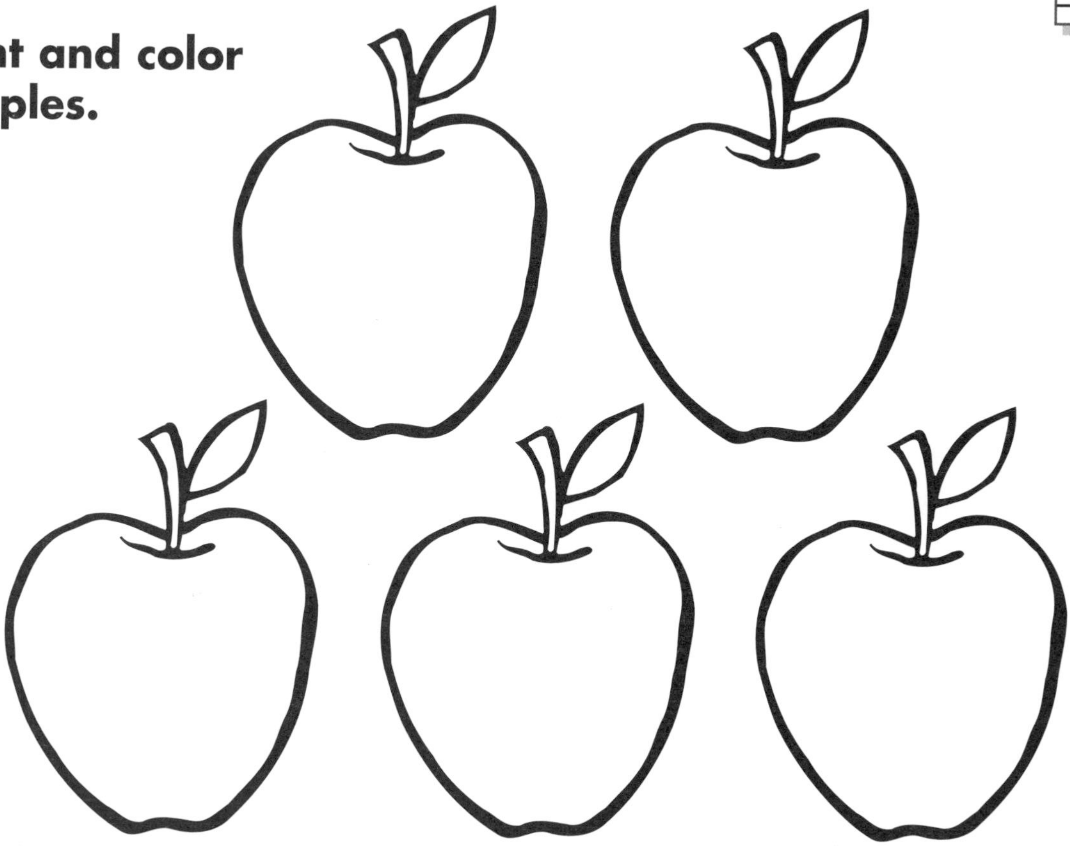

Name: _____

five

Circle the groups with 5.

Draw more butterflies to make 5.

Hooray for Six!

Let's clap six times
and touch the ground.
Let's jump six times
and spin around.
Let's stomp six times
and cheer and shout
for a wonderful number
we can't live without:
SIX!

Six Cheers for Ladybug

by Maria Fleming
Illustrated by Maxie Chambliss

SCHOLASTIC

Six candles with flames of gold.

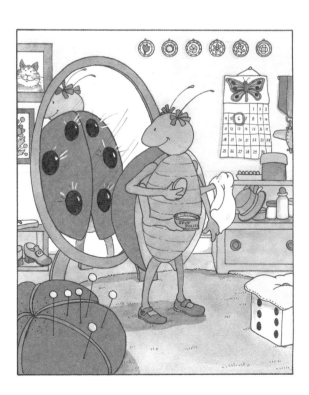

Ladybug shines her six black spots.

Six cheers for little Ladybug,
because today she's six years old!

A

She hurries down six stairs.

Six horns to blow.

B

Six hats to wear.

She puts six flowers in a vase.

The doorbell rings—six times, of course.
The party can begin!

Ladybug sets the table—
six plates, six cups, six spoons.

She pushes in six chairs.

Ladybug counts six presents
as her guests walk in.

C

She makes six party baskets.

She blows up six balloons.

D

Use with *Six Cheers for Ladybug*

Name: ____________________

6

six

Count and color 6 balloons.

Trace 6.

1

6

Write 6.

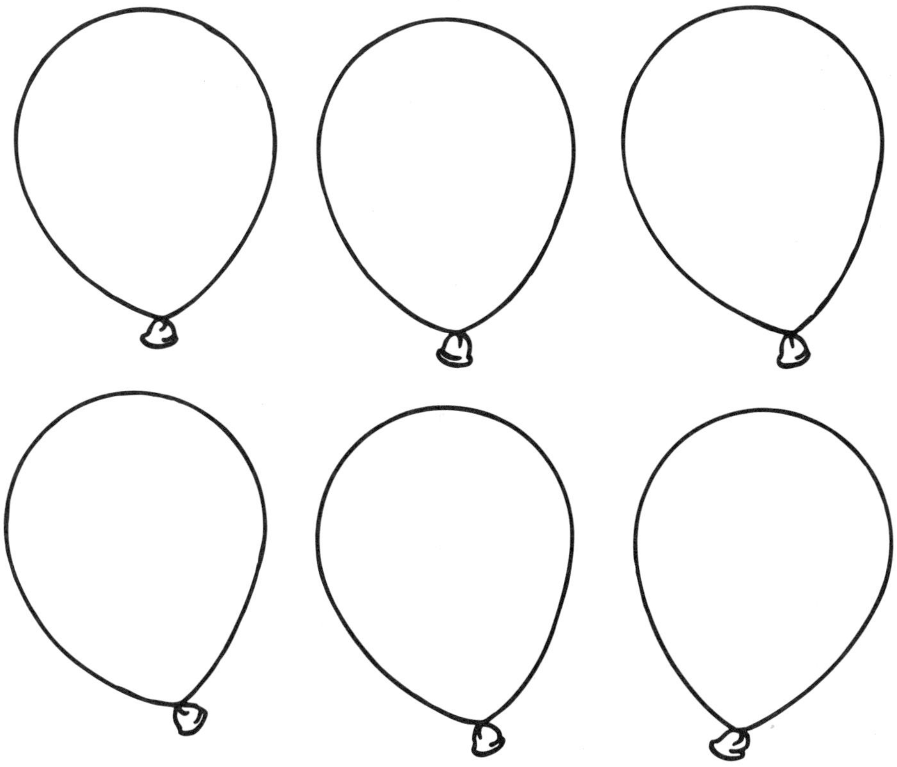

Name: _____

six

Circle the groups with 6.

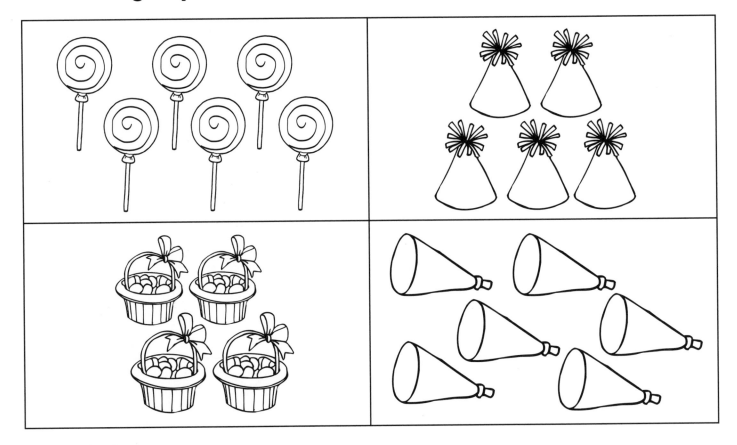

Draw 6 candles.

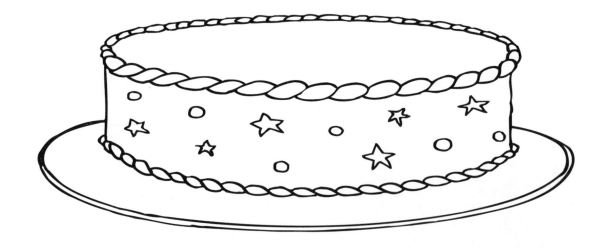

Hooray for Seven!

Let's clap seven times
and touch the ground.
Let's jump seven times
and spin around.
Let's stomp seven times
and cheer and shout
for a wonderful number
we can't live without:
SEVEN!

Seven Magic Hats

by Liza Charlesworth
Illustrated by Stephen Lewis

SCHOLASTIC

Then 1, 2, 3, 4, 5, 6, 7—

1, 2, 3, 4, 5, 6, 7—
seven magic hats had Kevin!

seven bellyaches had Kevin!

A

When he put them in the shower,

that made seven scrumptious cakes!

B

When he put them on some plates,

up sprang seven silly flowers!

When he plopped them on his shelves—

there sat seven teddy bears!

When he placed them on his chairs,

Poof! There soon were seven elves!

When he hung them on a door,

out stomped seven dinosaurs!

Name: _____

Count and color 7 hats.

seven

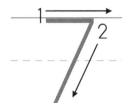

Trace 7.

Write 7.

63

Name: _____

seven

Circle the groups with 7.

Draw 7 apples on the plates.

Hooray for Eight!

Let's clap eight times
and touch the ground.
Let's jump eight times
and spin around.
Let's stomp eight times
and cheer and shout
for a wonderful number
we can't live without:
   EIGHT!

Eight Legs Are Great

by Liza Charlesworth
Illustrated by Jackie Snider

SCHOLASTIC

Eight legs are great to weave a web—
I made mine really high!

1, 2, 3, 4—
being a spider's super cool!
5, 6, 7, 8—
having eight legs sure is great!

A

1, 2, 3, 4—
being a spider's super cool!
5, 6, 7, 8—
having eight legs sure is great!

Eight legs are great to lead a cheer

and creep across a pie!

Eight legs are great to jitterbug

and ride a little bike!

Eight legs are great to swing and swing

and take a teeny hike!

Eight legs are great to run a race

and, then, to roller-skate!

C

Eight legs are great to jump a rope

and balance on a gate!

D

Name: _____

8

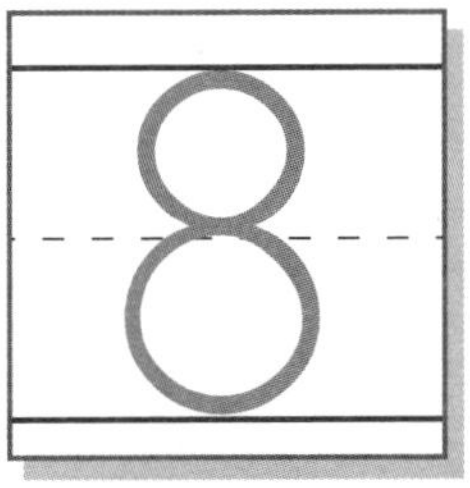

eight

Count and color 8 legs.

Trace 8.

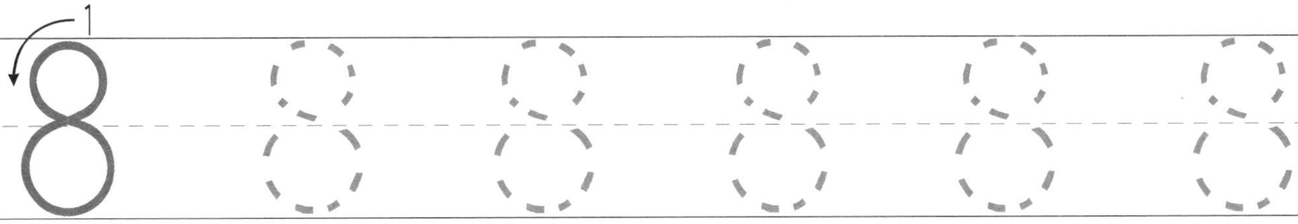

1

8 8 8 8 8 8

Write 8.

Name: _____

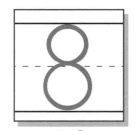

eight

Circle the groups with 8.

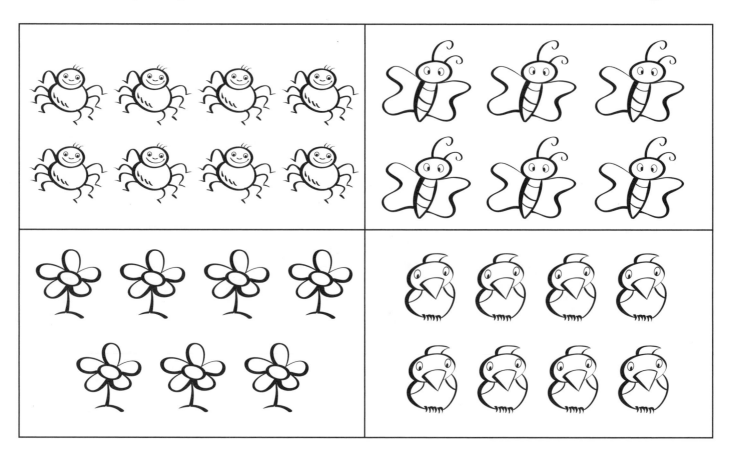

Draw 8 legs on the spider.

Hooray for Nine!

Let's clap nine times
and touch the ground.
Let's jump nine times
and spin around.
Let's stomp nine times
and cheer and shout
for a wonderful number
we can't live without:
    NINE!

Nine Bright Pennies

by Teddy Slater
Illustrated by Stephen Lewis

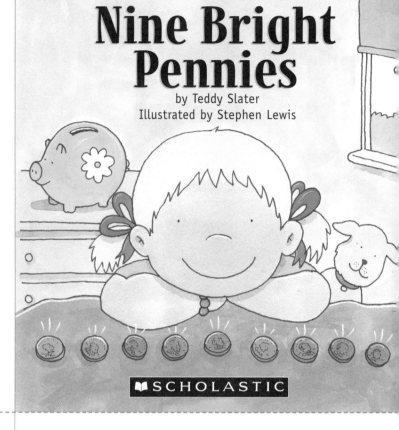

■ SCHOLASTIC

Nine bright pennies
don't seem like a lot.

Nine bright pennies don't seem like a lot.

A

But they're exactly enough
when you're thirsty and hot!

But that's all Maggie had,
and here's what she got:

B

Maggie sold the markers to her brother Reese,
who bought them all for a penny apiece.

and headed home with nine colored markers.

She hurried off to the candy store...

and strolled away with nine balloons.

Maggie traded the candy to her cousin Boris...

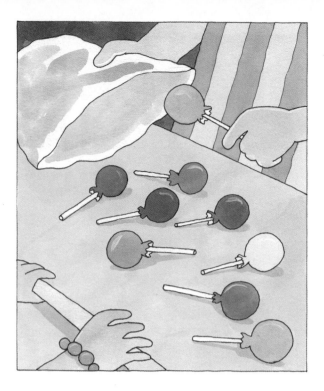

bought nine lollipops—
no less, no more.

C

She traded the balloons to Polly Parker...

and walked away with nine Stegosauruses.

D

Maggie traded those dinos to her
best friend June...

Name: _____

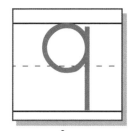

nine

Count and color 9 pennies.

Trace 9.

Write 9.

Name: _____

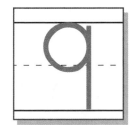

nine

Circle the groups with 9.

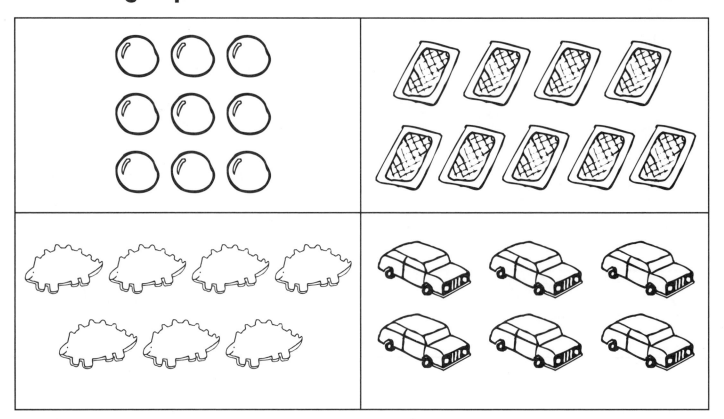

Draw more to make 9.

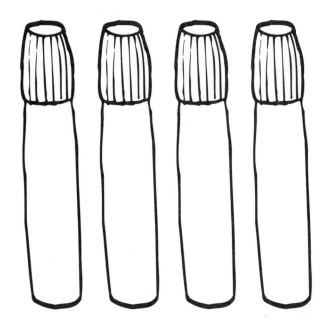

Hooray for Ten!

Let's clap ten times
and touch the ground.
Let's jump ten times
and spin around.
Let's stomp ten times
and cheer and shout
for a wonderful number
we can't live without:
TEN!

Ten Fingers Can!

by Liza Charlesworth
Illustrated by Anne Kennedy

SCHOLASTIC

Ten fingers can
count up to ten.

Ten fingers can
do many things!
They can touch and clap and wave.
They can dress in fancy rings.

A

Wow, that was fun!
Let's do it again!

Ten fingers can
catch a giant ball.

B

Ten fingers can
say, "I love you!"

Ten fingers can
learn to tie a shoe.

Ten fingers can
hug a favorite doll.

Ten fingers can
play and play and play!

Ten fingers can
launch a sailing ship.

Ten fingers can
button, snap, and zip.

C

Then, ten fingers can
put the toys away.

Ten fingers can
put on puppet shows.

D

Ten fingers can
tickle tiny toes.

Name: _____

10

ten

Count and color 10 fingers.

Trace 10.

Write 10.

Use with *Ten Fingers Can!*

Name: _____

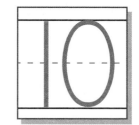

ten

Circle the groups with 10.

Color 10.

82

Hooray for Thirty!

Let's clap and tap
and touch the ground.
Let's jump and thump
and spin around.
Let's romp and stomp
and cheer and shout
for a wonderful number
we can't live without:
    THIRTY!

30 Mice Are Very Nice

by Maria Fleming
Illustrated by Hector Borlasca

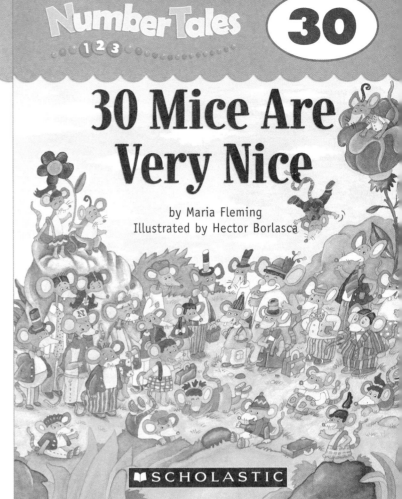

SCHOLASTIC

So Millie changed her mind and then
she sent her cousins home again.

Millie was a little mouse.
She lived alone in a great big house.

A

Now Millie is happy alone in her house—
just the right size for one little mouse.

Millie thought it might be nice
to live with lots of other mice.

B

Thirty mice wasn't nice at all.
Now Millie's house felt very small.

They were loud.

She called her cousins, "Come and stay."
They all moved in the very next day.

But thirty mice were quite a crowd.

by bus, balloon, train, plane, and car.

Her cousins came from near and far

They were messy.

Millie counted as they came
and called hello to each by name.

Thirty mice had come to stay.
Thirty mice! Hip-hip-hooray!

Name: _____

thirty

Count and color 30 mice.

Trace 30.

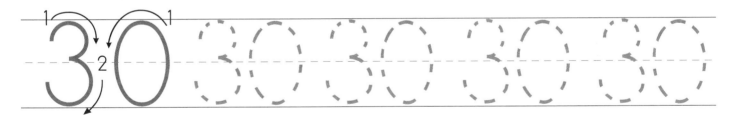

Write 30.

Name: _____

thirty

Circle the group with 30.

Draw more to make 30.

Hooray for 100!

Let's clap and tap
and touch the ground.
Let's jump and thump
and spin around.
Let's romp and stomp
and cheer and shout
for a wonderful number
we can't live without:
    ONE HUNDRED!

100 Wacky Wishes

by Liza Charlesworth
Illustrated by Kelly Kennedy

SCHOLASTIC

Or you could wish for 100 wishes

If you could wish for 100
of anything at all—
now, that would be amazing!
Wow, that would be a ball!

A

so you could wish some more!

13

You could wish for 100 butterflies

B

to grow out of the floor.

2

11

You could wish for 100 flowers

to flutter round your room

or 100 happy freckles

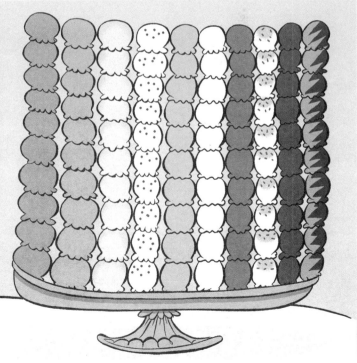

and a super-duper spoon!

or 100 scoops of ice cream

to decorate your face.

C

You could wish for 100 big balloons

to lift you into space

D

Name: _____

100

one hundred

**Count and color
100 blocks.**

Trace 100.

↓1 00 100 100 100

Write 100.

_____

- - - - - - - - - - - - - - - - - - - -

_____

_____

_____

Name: _____

100

one hundred

Count by 10's to 100.
Trace the numbers.

10   20   30   40   50

60   70   80   90   100

Hooray for Skip Counting!

Two—four—six—eight—
we can count by twos,
let's celebrate!

Let's clap by twos
and tap by twos.
Let's jump by twos
and thump by twos.

Two—four—six—eight—
skip counting is really great!

The Ants Go Marching Two by Two

by Liza Charlesworth
Illustrated by Maxie Chambliss

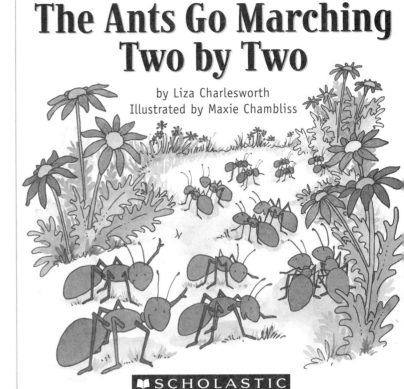

■ SCHOLASTIC

They're marching high. They're marching low.
Count them again as they go, go, go.

The ants go marching two by two. Hurrah! Hurrah!
Underneath a sky of blue. Hurrah! Hurrah!

A

And they all go marching along, singing a song, waving so long. Bye! Bye! Bye!

Two ants, four ants, six ants, eight— march along the garden gate.

B

Their fun is done, so toodleloo! Hurrah! Hurrah!

The ants are marching two by two. Hurrah! Hurrah!

And they all go marching out, stomping about, having fun in the sun. Tra-la-la!

Watch them chomp, chew, and munch,

Marching past a row of plants. Hurrah! Hurrah!

Ten, twelve, fourteen, sixteen ants. Hurrah! Hurrah!

C

making crumbs as they crunch. Yum! Yum! Yum!

Here come more ants—eighteen, twenty.
Twenty ants! Twenty is plenty...

D

to enjoy a picnic lunch.

Name: _____

Count by 2's. Color the ants.

Trace the numbers.

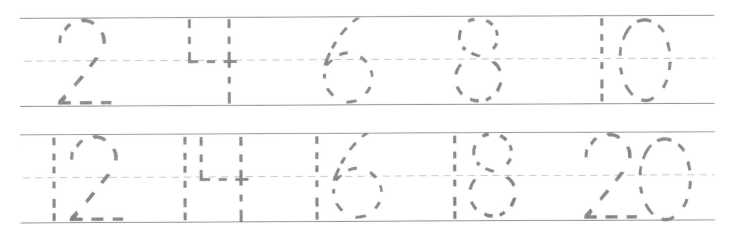

Name: _____

Count by 2's. Circle the number.

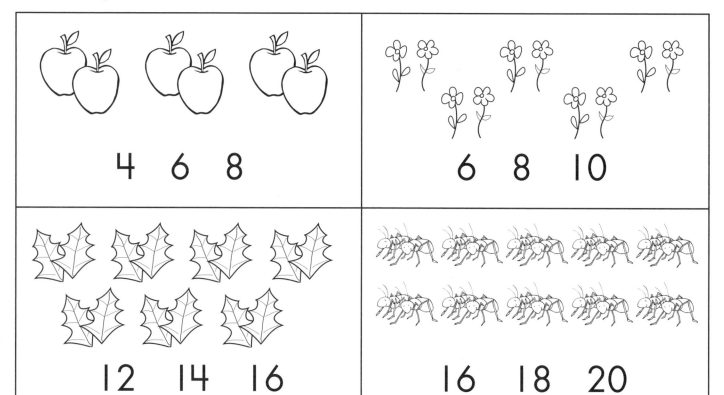

Count by 2's. Write the missing numbers.

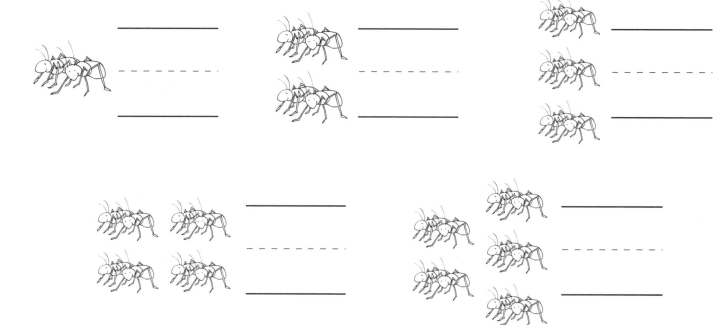

Hooray for Addition!

Let's clap and tap
and touch the ground.
Let's jump and thump
and spin around.
Let's romp and stomp
and cheer and shout
for something
we can't live without:
ADDITION!

The Happy Hippos

by Liza Charlesworth
Illustrated by Daniel J. Mahoney

SCHOLASTIC

they're playing till day's done.

One happy hippo practicing Kung-Fu.

1 + 1 + 1 + 1 + 1 = 5 happy hippos having tons of fun!

13

A

Can I join you?

"Can I join you?" asked her brother Lou.

2

They're running, rolling, riding...

B

Five happy hippos rumbling in the sun.

One hippo plus one hippo, that equals two.

Four happy hippos doing fancy dives.
"Can I join you?" asked cousin Clive.

Two hippos plus one hippo, that equals three!

Two happy hippos racing round a tree.
"Can I join you?" asked their neighbor Lee.

4

Four hippos plus one hippo, that equals five.

9

C

Three happy hippos playing grocery store.
"Can I join you?" asked their friend Theodore.

6

D

Three hippos plus one hippo, that equals four.

7

Name: _____

Add. Write how many.

_____   _____   **in all**
_____

- - - - - -   **+**   - - - - - -   **=**   - - - - - -

_____   _____   _____

   **in all**
_____   _____

- - - - - -   **+**   - - - - - -   **=**   - - - - - -

_____   _____   _____

_____   _____   **in all**
_____   _____

- - - - - -   **+**   - - - - - -   **=**   - - - - - -

_____   _____   _____

   **in all**
_____   _____

- - - - - -   **+**   - - - - - -   **=**   - - - - - -

_____   _____   _____

Name: _____

Add. Write how many.

      **in all**

_____   _____   _____

- - - - - - - - - **+** - - - - - - - - - **=** - - - - - - - - -

_____   _____   _____

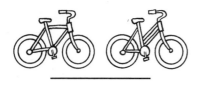      **in all**

_____   _____   _____

- - - - - - - - - **+** - - - - - - - - - **=** - - - - - - - - -

_____   _____   _____

   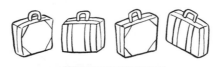   **in all**

_____   _____   _____

- - - - - - - - - **+** - - - - - - - - - **=** - - - - - - - - -

_____   _____   _____

      **in all**

_____   _____   _____

- - - - - - - - - **+** - - - - - - - - - **=** - - - - - - - - -

_____   _____   _____

Hooray for Subtraction!

Let's clap and tap
and touch the ground.
Let's jump and thump
and spin around.
Let's romp and stomp
and cheer and shout
for something
we can't live without:
 SUBTRACTION!

14

Monkey's Missing Bananas

by Liza Charlesworth
Illustrated by Brenda Sexton

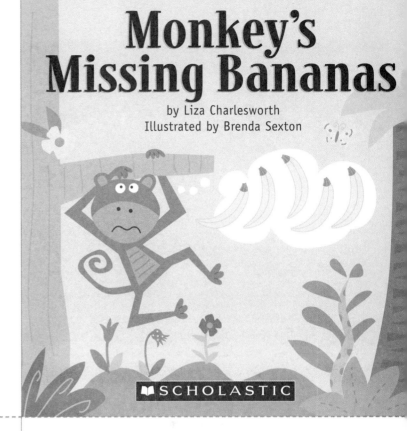

SCHOLASTIC

"Who munched all my bananas?"
he said, scratching his head.

12

Five big bananas were sitting in the sun,
but along came a cranky crocodile...

1

But he soon got tired of thinking
and just picked more instead.

A

and—SNAP!—he gobbled one.
$5 - 1 = 4$

No big bananas were sitting in the sun,
which surprised the silly monkey
who'd laid them out for lunch.

And—ROAR!—he gobbled one.
1 – 1 = 0

Four big bananas were sitting in the sun,
but along came a slinky python...

and—SNORT!—he gobbled one.
2 – 1 = 1

Three big bananas were sitting in the sun,
but along came a laughing hyena...

and—SSSSSSS!—he gobbled one.
4 – 1 = 3

and—HEE-HEE!—he gobbled one.
3 – 1 = 2

One big banana was sitting in the sun,
but along came a ferocious lion...

Two big bananas were sitting in the sun,
but along came a giant rhino...

Name: _____

Subtract. Write how many are left.

$5 - 1 =$ _____

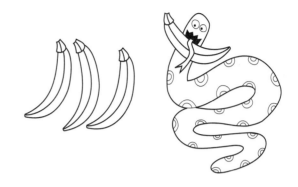

$4 - 1 =$ _____

$3 - 1 =$ _____

$2 - 1 =$ _____

Name: _____

Subtract.

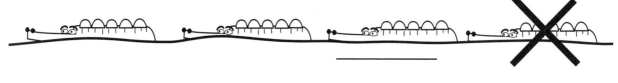

4 − 1 = _____

_____

5 − 2 = _____

_____

4 − 3 = _____

_____

3 − 1 = _____

_____

Name: _____

Count. Draw lines to match.

 4

2

 1

5

3

Name: _____

Count. Draw lines to match.

8	
6	
7	
10	
9	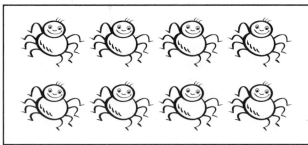

Name: _____

Hundreds Chart

1	2	3	4	5	6	7	8	9	10
11	12	13	14	15	16	17	18	19	20
21	22	23	24	25	26	27	28	29	30
31	32	33	34	35	36	37	38	39	40
41	42	43	44	45	46	47	48	49	50
51	52	53	54	55	56	57	58	59	60
61	62	63	64	65	66	67	68	69	70
71	72	73	74	75	76	77	78	79	80
81	82	83	84	85	86	87	88	89	90
91	92	93	94	95	96	97	98	99	100

Flash Cards

1 one	☆
2 two	☆ ☆
3 three	☆ ☆ ☆
4 four	☆ ☆ ☆ ☆
5 five	☆ ☆ ☆ ☆ ☆

Flash Cards

6 six	☆ ☆ ☆ ☆ ☆ ☆
7 seven	☆ ☆ ☆ ☆ ☆ ☆ ☆
8 eight	☆ ☆ ☆ ☆ ☆ ☆ ☆ ☆
9 nine	☆ ☆ ☆ ☆ ☆ ☆ ☆ ☆ ☆
10 ten	☆ ☆ ☆ ☆ ☆ ☆ ☆ ☆ ☆ ☆

Spinner 1 Cut out the arrow and attach it with a brass fastener.

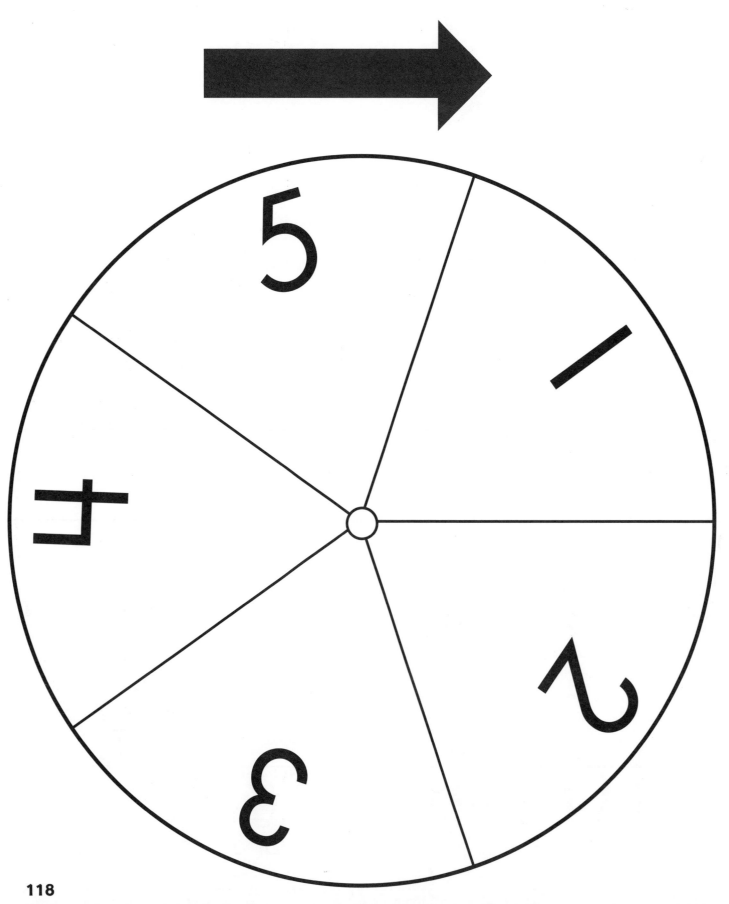

Spinner 2   Cut out the arrow and attach it with a brass fastener.

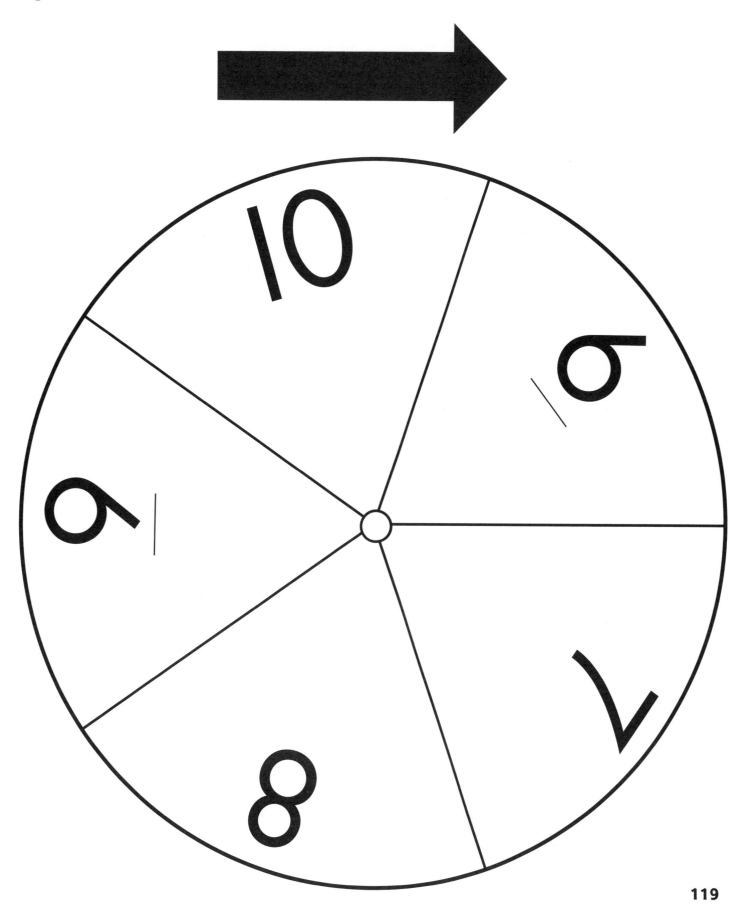

Notes